UNDERSTANDING THE DARK SIDE: WESTERN DEMONOLOGY, SATANIC PANICS AND ALIEN ABDUCTION

Christopher Partridge

Professor of Contemporary Religion

CW00819495

An Inaugural Lecture
Delivered at University College Chester
on 24 June 2004

Chester Academic Press

First published 2006
by Chester Academic Press
Corporate Communications
University of Chester
Parkgate Road
Chester CH1 4BJ

Printed and bound in the UK by the
Learning Resources Print Unit
University of Chester
Cover designed by the
Learning Resources Graphics Team
University of Chester

A catalogue record for this publication is available from
the British Library

UNDERSTANDING THE DARK SIDE: WESTERN DEMONOLOGY, SATANIC PANICS AND ALIEN ABDUCTION[1]

Introduction

The contemporary interest in UFOs can be traced back to the 24th June 1947, the day when Kenneth Arnold, a businessman from Boise, Idaho, reported sighting ten shining discs flying over the Cascade Mountains when flying his private plane near Mount Rainier in western Washington. According to Arnold, "... they flew like a saucer would if you skipped it across the water" (see Baker, 2000, p. v). Misquoted, the sighting was reported as Arnold's encounter with "flying saucers". Whilst there had been previous modern sightings of, for example, "balls of fire" accompanying planes during the Second World War (nicknamed "foo fighters") or cigar- and disc-shaped objects in the sky (such as the wave of Scandinavian "ghost rocket" sightings in 1946), these tended to be sporadic and vague. Moreover, as Robert Bartholomew and George Howard have shown, before 1947 "... there is not a single recorded episode involving mass sightings of saucer-like objects" (1998, p. 189). It was Arnold's flying saucers that

---

[1] I would like to thank those who commented on an earlier version of this lecture, which was delivered as a paper at the 2003 British Association for the Study of Religions Conference. I would also like to thank Robert Segal for his helpful comments on a later draft. A slightly revised version of the lecture was published under the title "Alien demonology: The Christian roots of the malevolent extraterrestrial in UFO religions and abduction spiritualities", in *Religion*, 34 (2004), 163-189.

both began the modern waves of sightings and also ushered UFOs into the popular consciousness. The interest in Arnold's story was immediate and massive: "A Gallup poll taken on August 19, 1947, revealed that while one out of two Americans had heard of the Marshall Plan, nine out of ten had heard about the saucers" (Lagrange, 2000, p. 34). By the end of that year, 850 UFO sightings were reported in America alone.

As to *why* the interest in UFOs has been particularly prevalent since the 1950s, several theories might be posited. Firstly, the enormous media interest in UFO sightings was certainly a factor. Secondly, it is difficult to underestimate the significance of the tension and sense of insecurity engendered by the Cold War and the threat of an East–West nuclear conflict. Whether one agrees with Carl Jung's particular psychological thesis or not (see Segal, 2003), his identification of this context as important in understanding why people might look beyond the planet for help is surely correct (Jung, 1969, pp. 25-26). UFO groups and contactees of the 1950s claimed to receive messages from highly spiritually evolved, morally superior, technologically advanced, benevolent beings with a deep salvific concern for a humanity bent on the nuclear destruction of the planet (see Festinger, Riecken, & Schachter, 1964, pp. 46-7; Helland, 2003; Partridge, 2003, p. 12). Thirdly, this was a period both of enormous technological advance and also of religious decline. Therefore, on the one hand, salvation was less likely to be conceived in traditionally religious terms and, on the other hand, as Jung argued, this was the genesis of the Space Age, when people were beginning seriously to imagine life beyond the confines of their terrestrial home: the corollary of such speculation being the inhabitants of other worlds thinking similar thoughts and visiting us (Segal, 2003, p. 317). It is, therefore, of little surprise that the political and cultural environment of the late 1940s and the 1950s engendered a fascination with UFOs and alien visitation.

It is also worth noting at this stage that the theosophical tradition[2] has proved to be enormously significant in the history of UFO religion. The reason for this can be found in theosophical speculation about other worlds and extraterrestrial civilisations. H. P. Blavatsky,

---

[2] Arguably, "theosophy" can be traced back through Plotinus, Ammonius Saccas, and Plato to Pythagorean Greece. It has since surfaced periodically in Western esotericism, being, as Emily Sellon and Renée Weber point out, " ...most legitimately associated with figures such as Meister Eckhart, Giordano Bruno, Emanuel Swedenborg, and Jacob Boehme" (Sellon & Weber, 1992, p. 311). Following a period of obscurity, it was then revived at the end of the nineteenth century by the Russian occultist Helena Petrovna Blavatsky and an American, Henry Steel Olcott, who, in 1875, founded the Theosophical Society in New York. Most contemporary theosophists will identify the life and work of Blavatsky as the source of the modern theosophical tradition. She published two major works, *Isis Unveiled* (1877) and *The Secret Doctrine* (1888), and several more accessible volumes, all of which have sold widely and have remained in print. The influence of the Theosophical Society has been wide and significant, it being one of the principal organisations responsible for popularising both Western esotericism and the core teachings of Hinduism and Buddhism in the West. Although there were many disputes about theosophical doctrines and subsequent secessions, significant thinkers within the alternative tradition, such as Alice Bailey, Annie Besant, Christmas Humphries, Rudolf Steiner, Krishnamurti, and Guy and Edna Ballard, including many contemporary "New Age" spiritual leaders, such as Elizabeth Clare Prophet of the Church Universal and Triumphant, are fundamentally indebted to Blavatsky and the Theosophical Society (see Tingay, 2000). As to the basic doctrines, these are summed up well by Kevin Tingay: " ...a scheme of spiritual evolution that underlies physical evolution. Human beings seen as the embodiments of sparks of the Divine, which journey back to their origin through a series of incarnations. The law of karma is the mechanism that controls the circumstances of each successive life. Among those who reach a high stage of moral and spiritual development are those [ascended] masters who attempt to assist their "younger brethren" through the work of the Theosophical Society and other movements" (Tingay, 2004, p. 321).

the founder of modern theosophy, had speculated about the Venusian "Lords of the Flame", which were, according to Charles Leadbeater's interpretation of the concept (1912), of the highest rank in the hierarchy of ascended masters. Subsequently, leaders within the tradition, such as Guy Ballard, the founder of the "I AM" Religious Activity, claimed, under the pseudonym Godfre Ray King, to have met twelve Venusians who revealed Venus to be home to a race of technologically and spiritually advanced beings (1934). Hence, it is unsurprising that UFO religion has been dominated by those from within the theosophical tradition. This is, for example, true of both George Adamski, the first and arguably the most influential contactee (see Adamski, 1949), and also George King, the founder (in 1956) of the oldest UFO religion, the Aetherius Society (see Wallis, 1974; Smith, 2003).

The above political, cultural and religious factors ensured that the process of the sacralisation of the extraterrestrial produced, in the early period, an understanding of the alien as a fundamentally benevolent, messianic figure. The extraterrestrial emerged as a spiritually and intellectually advanced being, seeking to intervene salvifically in the affairs of a morally and spiritually inferior, if not bankrupt, race, bent on the destruction of its planet. Indeed, just as UFO religion has its origins in theosophy, so the extraterrestrial in much UFO spirituality is fundamentally indebted to the concept of the ascended master developed within that tradition, particularly the "I AM" movement (see Stupple, 1984; Partridge, 2003, pp. 7-21). It is not surprising, therefore, that, until recently, there has been comparatively little reference outside popular culture to the extraterrestrial as an essentially malevolent being. Although the demonised extraterrestrial has not been entirely absent, the emphasis has been very clearly on the alien as space saviour, or, to

4

use Jung's term, "technological angel" (1969). However, in recent years, a shift has taken place in some religious (and also conspiracy) discourse. Following most religious traditions, a demonology has begun to evolve in order to take account of moral evil, suffering, frustrated religious expectations, perceived temptation, and the general unsatisfactoriness of life. This lecture is an analysis of the origins, nature and function of such demonologies. However, in order to provide such an analysis, we first need to begin with some discussion of Western demonology *per se*, for, as I will argue, this is the soil in which these contemporary demonologies have their roots.

Demonology in the West

Personifications of evil in the form of demons, devils, spirits and malign entities can be found across the religious spectrum. Whilst the term "demon" has acquired a specifically evil connotation, the Classical Greek *daimōn* (meaning 'spirit'), from which it is derived through late Medieval Latin, was used of any malevolent or benevolent spirit (*agathos daimōn*), deified hero, demigod or ancestor spirit that mediated between the transcendent and temporal realms (see Russell, 1977, pp. 142-44; Bolt, 1996). Over time, however, such demons gradually came to be understood as malevolent. Hence, by the late Greco-Roman period, the term *daimonia* was specifically applied to evil spirits, the main work of which was to frustrate, to harm and, particularly, to tempt humans into sin (see Russell, 1977, pp. 34, 142; Forsyth, 1987, p. 293). Indeed, the Stoic systematisation of late-Platonic demonology, which understood the *daimonia* to exist in an ontological level between the gods and humanity, is reflected in 1 Enoch 15 and 2 Enoch 29: 5, where fallen angels are described as hovering in the lower air (see Galloway, 1951,

p. 25; Russell, 1977, pp. 191ff.; Forsyth, 1987, pp. 160-181). It is this understanding of the term *daimonium* that is adopted in the Septuagint, the New Testament and the early Church.

We will see that reference to demons can be found in the Hebrew Bible: e.g., *Aza'zel* (Leviticus 16: 8-10: see Russell, 1977, pp. 176, 191, 206; Forsyth, 1987, p. 178); *lîlîth* (Isaiah 34: 14: see Trachtenberg, 1970, pp. 28, 36-37; Russell, 1977, p. 215); the *shédîm*, to whom people sacrificed their sons and their daughters (Psalms 106: 37: see Trachtenberg, 1970, p. 27); and, of course, the Satan figure (1 Chronicles 21; Job 1, 2; Zechariah 3: 1: see Forsyth, 1987, pp. 107-123; Nielsen, 1998). Also, some of the basic characteristics of a good–evil dualism can be traced back to Iranian Zoroastrianism (see Russell, 1977, pp. 98-121, 217-220). Yet it is not until the second and first centuries BCE, during the apocalyptic period, that a sophisticated demonology began to evolve within Jewish theology. As Jewish apocalyptic demonology developed, demons were increasingly understood to interfere spiritually with humans, tempting them into sin and thereby disrupting their relationship with God (see Russell, 1977, pp. 191ff.). The *daimonia* sought to deceive with false revelations, to pervert true divine revelation, and to confuse. More significantly, there evolved the notion of a single source, or unitary concept of evil. There was a "… movement of thought away from the explanation of evil in terms of numerous capricious spirits operating at random, towards an explanation in terms of a hierarchy or unified body of evil [which] reaches its climax in the New Testament" (Ling, 1961, p. 9). This is supported by Jeffrey Burton Russell, who argues, firstly, that Satan is "… the malignant, destructive aspect of Yahweh … subtracted from him and ascribed to a different spiritual power" (Russell, 1977, p. 183). Secondly, he shows how the apocalyptic writers developed the idea of the Devil as

"... a spiritual being personifying the origin and essence of evil" and as the leader of the demonised "Watcher angels" (Russell, 1977, p. 188).

Certainly, in the Hebrew Bible Satan is not the demonic figure he becomes in apocalyptic literature (see Kluger, 1967). Indeed, Satan is one of the "members of the court of heaven", one of the *benē 'elōhīm*, a "son of God" (Job 1: 6). The Book of Job in particular describes Satan as a being who works closely with Yahweh as his agent in the testing of Job (see Nielsen, 1998, pp. 59-105). According to Russell, Satan as a son of God has his origins in Canaanite religion:

> In Canaan these "sons" are gods, manifestations of the divine principle. Clearly, the original idea in Hebrew religion was that Yahweh was surrounded by a pantheon comparable to that of Zeus or Wotan. The idea of a pantheon was displeasing to strict monotheism, and the *banim* (*bene ha'elohim*) became shadowy figures. Yet they retained an important function of separating the evil aspect of the divine nature from the good. (Russell, 1977, p. 184)

Kirsten Nielsen explains the relationship between God and Satan more literally in terms of father and son:

> At the beginning father and son are together, but at a certain time their paths separate.... Satan in the book of Job [is] the son of God who for some time roamed the earth.... He lived among the other sons of God, close to his father. There is nothing to indicate that he was denied this position after he had tested Job, neither was there a revolt against his father or any fall from the heavenly to the earthly. (Nielsen, 1998, p. 156)

Only in later Jewish legend do we find Satan banished from heaven.

Of particular interest to later apocalyptic writers (and to contemporary UFO religionists) is Genesis 6: 1-4, which describes the *benē 'elōhīm* descending to earth and having sexual relations with human women, the progeny of which was a race of giants known as the *nephīlīm*.

> When men began to multiply on the face of the ground, and daughters were born to them, the sons of God saw that the daughters of men were fair; and they took to wife such of them as they chose. Then the Lord said, "My spirit shall not abide in man for ever, for he is flesh, but his days shall be a hundred and twenty years". The Nephilim were on the earth in those days, and also afterward, when the sons of God came in to the daughters of men, and they bore children to them. These were the mighty men that were of old, the men of renown. (Genesis 6: 1-4)

Tracing this back to Canaanite mythology, Claus Westermann argues that it belongs to a distinct cycle of relatively common narratives that deal with the sexual union of deities and humans (Westermann, 1994, p. 369). While there is much scholarly debate as to the meaning of "sons of God" in Genesis 6 (see Russell, 1977, pp. 174 ff.; Westermann, 1994, pp. 371-372; Clines, 1996; Nielsen, 1998, pp. 156-183), the oldest and most common interpretation within the Christian tradition is, perhaps not surprisingly, "angel". That said, because of the particular baggage that term carries, Gordon Wenham prefers the more ambiguous term "spirit", recognising that such "sons of the gods" may be benevolent or malevolent (Wenham, 1987, p. 140). Less convincing are the arguments of those, such as Umberto Cassuto, who insist that the term should be interpreted as "angels ... of a degraded type" (Westermann, 1994, p. 372). This understanding simply reflects post apocalyptic Christian interpretations. Justin Martyr, for example, is very clear that they were in fact "fallen angels" and that demons are the product of their unnatural union with human women (see Kelly, 1977, p. 167). Later in Christian history, Martin Luther reiterates the early Christian belief that the "sons of the gods" are fallen angels and the *nephīlīm* demons (see Luther, 1543/1960, pp. 10-12). These views, however, are clearly influenced by apocalyptic speculation.

One of the most influential early apocalyptic accounts of the fall of the *benē 'elōhīm* and their *nephīlīm* progeny appears in 1 Enoch. Whereas in Genesis it is not clear that these beings are particularly evil, in the apocalyptic literature they reveal their evil nature in their lust for human women. Referred to as "the Watcher angels", 1 Enoch also identifies their leader, Semyaz (1 Enoch 6: 3):

> The decision takes the form of a conspiracy, in which they enter into a mutual obligation under the leadership of Semyaz. Their leader is well aware that their plan is contrary to God's will. He therefore wishes them to undertake a mutual obligation, so that the others do not suddenly abandon the plan and leave him on his own, and "I alone will become responsible for this great sin". Then all 200 angels take an oath to stand together as concerns responsibility, and they descend to the summit of Mount Hermon, divided into units of ten, each with its leader, as if they were about to embark on a campaign of war. (Nielsen, 1998, p. 161)

9

(Interestingly, we are told that, having had sexual intercourse with human women, the "angels" teach them magic charms and incantations; a point which has not gone unnoticed by those in Christian history seeking to construct a demonology of the witch.) We are told that the *nephilīm* offspring, a race of giants, eat all the food gathered by humans, leaving them to starve, and, eventually, turn on the humans themselves in a cannibalistic rampage. Furthermore, Azazel, one of the Watchers, who is later identified with Satan (see Russell, 1977, p. 206), teaches the humans to make weapons of war, as well as introducing them to jewellery, costly gems and dyes, all of which lead to greed, violence and vanity. Eventually, God responds by sending the four archangels, Michael, Uriel, Raphael, and Gabriel, to slay the giants; although their malign spirits remain to "… afflict, oppress, destroy, attack, do battle, and work destruction on earth" (1 Enoch 15: 1). Raphael is also instructed to bind Azazel and cast him into an outer darkness, where he is to remain until the day of judgment, when he shall be "sent into the fire" (1 Enoch 10: 5-7).

It is also in the apocalyptic writings that we see pride ascribed to the Devil. Enoch applies Isaiah's satirical song about the King of Babylon, the "bright morning star" now "fallen from heaven" (Isaiah 14: 12-15), to Satan, who has been cast out because of the sin of pride. (Hence, he acquired the name Lucifer, meaning "light-bearer", a name used of the morning star.) Satan having rebelled, the distance between God and the Devil gradually widens in apocalyptic literature. No longer is Satan God's agent in the world, accusing and harming humans with divine permission. Apocalyptic developments push toward a dualism in which God is wholly dissociated from evil, this being the Devil's business.

The Lord is closely associated with ethical good and the Devil with ethical evil. The Devil is the personification of sin, and he commands at his right and left hands the spirits of wrath, hatred and lying. He is lord of fornication, war, bloodshed, exile, death, panic and destruction. He tempts humankind into error.... He rules over the souls of the wicked.... (Russell, 1977, pp. 209-211)

While in later Jewish thought, as Joshua Trachtenberg comments, the Devil "... never played a very prominent role ... as a distinct personality", being "... little more than an allegory, whose moral was the prevalence of sin" (Trachtenberg, 1943, p. 19), this is not the case in Christianity. The apocalyptic writings provide substantial foundations for the construction of a complex demonology. All the key themes, from the sexual sin of the *benē 'elōhīm* to the pride of Lucifer, from the imprisonment of demons beneath the earth in the pit (or in the "lower atmosphere") to their continuing interference with humans in order to tempt them away from God and, finally, to their demise "... at the end of the world when the Messiah comes" (Russell, 1977, p. 207), are carefully developed in Christian demonologies. Furthermore, Jewish apocalyptic demonology has another importance, in that there is a shift away from the prophetic insistence on interior human responsibility for one's own sin, to an exterior source *other than* God. That is to say, it provides a way of explaining human evil which does not, on the one hand, require God as its source and yet, on the other hand, does not need to explain any ills and failings that befall individuals as a consequence of previous sinful action. Hence, as Bernard McGinn's study of the history of the Antichrist shows, although there is an external-internal polarity throughout Christian history, more attention is given to the notion of an external foe (McGinn, 1994, p. 4). Indeed, although many Christian thinkers, certainly in the modern period, have tended to focus on the interior nature of evil, their perennial human fascination with an objective source of evil still persists. Certainly central to much early and medieval Christian theology was the belief that, although all are responsible for their own sins, they are also continually subject to the advances and corruption of personal demons, all of which operate as the agents of Satan. This is, again, very clear in the theology of Justin, for whom devils and demons were understood to be "... swarming everywhere ... [obsessing] men's souls and bodies, infecting them with vice and corruption" (Kelly, 1977, p. 167; cf. Justin, in Stevenson, 1987, p. 60). Likewise, the desert fathers, whose influence continued throughout the Middle Ages, believed hordes of malign demons populated the world, taking every opportunity both to *obsess* human beings: i.e., to attack and influence them from without, as well as to *possess* some unfortunate individuals: i.e., as Augustine puts it, "[to] inhabit their bodies" and seize them from within (Augustine, ca. 413-426/1945, p. 326). Indeed, according to Athanasius's *Life of Antony*, believing the desert to be the abode of demons,[3] Antony went there "... to do battle with the powers of evil" (see Russell, 1981, pp. 172-177). Alone in the desert, he was "... attacked by demons, who tried various devices to distract him from the holy life" (Hall, 1991, p. 174). However, again, whilst all manner of harm to humans and animals, as well as natural disasters, were understood to be the result of demonic activity, a demon's ultimate aim was to

---

[3] The desert (or wilderness) was commonly understood to be populated by demons. For example, this is the abode of *Aza'zel* (Leviticus 16: 18) and, of course, is the place where Jesus was led by the Spirit to be tempted by the Devil (Matthew 4: 1). See Russell, 1981, pp. 149-185.

corrupt the soul, to tempt, and to disrupt a person's relationship with God. Temptation is, as one theologian put it, "... the invasion of Satan's power into the world of creation.... [It is] seduction, leading astray" (Bonhoeffer, 1955, p. 24).

Jewish apocalyptic demonology shaped Western demonologies, fundamentally distinguishing them from those of pagan religions (see Jones & Pennick, 1995, p. 60). Of particular significance is the clear understanding that: "Satan embodies the ultimate truth behind the profuse demonology of popular thought" (Ling, 1961, p. 12). This led to the incorporation of folk beliefs into a systematic demonology. For example, Karen Louise Jolly notes, in her fine study of popular religion in tenth and eleventh century England, that:

> Amoral creatures such as elves were gradually "demonised" to fit the Good–Evil paradigm of the Christian moral universe. This process enhanced their similarity to demons. Their invisibility, their malicious attacks, and the need to "charm" them away all took on new meaning in Christian eyes so that elves began to resemble the fallen angels who seek to inflict internal and permanent harm on humans and their works, demons for Christian ritual to exorcise. (Jolly, 1996, p. 136)

Individual events and disturbances experienced on the plane of history are, on the one hand, understood as particularised demonic activity and, on the other, are projected into eternity, being fundamentally related to cosmic principalities and powers and the satanic attempt to thwart God's ultimate, salvific purpose.

As demonology evolved through the Middle Ages and, as is clearly evident in Heinrich Kramer's influential witch-hunter's manual of 1487, the *Malleus Maleficarum*, it focused increasingly on obsession, possession, and demonic alliances with humans (see Bailey, 2003; this study focuses on the medieval Dominican theologian Johannes Nider, whose demonology greatly influenced Kramer). As well as being the source of evil, as Jean La Fontaine comments:

> Satan and his demons were believed to have human allies and servants.... One of the ways in which devils, or the Devil, were believed to associate with human beings was in lending them extra-human powers to perform acts that were beyond the range of human beings.... By the Middle Ages, learned magicians were suspected of summoning and using demons by their magic in order to exchange their souls for magical powers in Faustian contracts. (La Fontaine, 1999, p. 85. See also Briggs, 1996, p. 3)

That said, it is important to note that, whilst this could be true of witches in many cultures, in that witchcraft is in no sense limited to European thought (see Parrinder, 1963; Bowie, 2000, pp. 219-258), it was only in the Middle Ages that, as Keith Thomas argues:

> ... a new element was added to the European concept of witchcraft which was to distinguish it from the witch-beliefs of other primitive peoples. This was the notion that the witch owed her powers to having made a deliberate pact with the Devil. (Thomas, 1973, p. 521)

(As noted above, such beliefs, of course, can be supported with reference to the apocalyptic interpretation of Genesis 6: 1-4. Moreover, we will see that it is also difficult to avoid the striking similarities with many contemporary alien abduction narratives.)

Whilst in the modern period the belief in demons retreated significantly before the forces of rationalism and empiricism, it did not, and has not, disappeared entirely (see Russell, 1986). Even if demons no longer seemed credible to many, particularly as most of their various works could be explained quite easily by modern science and medicine, the belief and popular interest in Satan has continued.

Of particular note in the modern West has been a series of "satanic panics" (see Richardson, Best, & Bromley, 1991; Victor, 1993). Working explicitly with traditional Christian demonology, in the early 1980s several lines of conspiratorial thought converged (see Victor, 1993, p. 8), the results of which were, on the one hand, graphic claims being made about subversive, satanic activity and, on the other, a popular movement which bore more than a passing resemblance to the pre-modern witch craze. In brief, these claims assert that:

> ... there exists a secret organization, or network, of criminals who worship Satan and who are engaged in the pornography business, forced prostitution, and drug dealing. These criminals also engage in the sexual abuse and torture of children in an effort to brainwash them into becoming life-long Devil worshippers. In their Devil worshipping rituals, these criminals kill and sacrifice infants, and sometimes adults, and commit cannibalism with the body parts. They kidnap children for ritual sacrifice and commit random murders of indigents. They actively try to recruit into their secret groups teenagers who dabble in occult magic. (Victor, 1993, p. 3-4)

15

That many of these themes emerge virtually unchanged in abduction narratives and alien demonologies is significant. Indeed, spreading the net more widely, whether one considers the demonologies within some sections of the Christian community (see, for example, Wright, 1996), the anti-cult world views which have inspired contemporary satanic panics, the supernaturalism of popular culture (such as the satanic chic of contemporary heavy metal) or, as we will see, the demonisation of the extraterrestrial, it is clear that they are all drawing from a common pool of myths and ideas that can be traced back through the periods of the witch-craze and the Middle Ages to early Christian thought and, ultimately, to Jewish apocalypticism.

Popular Culture, Abduction Narratives, and the Technological Demon

From Johann Heinrich Füssli's[4] disturbing painting *The Nightmare* (1782), which depicts an incubus squatting on the stomach of a sleeping woman, to Ridley Scott's *Alien* (1979), modern Western artists, writers and philosophers have drunk deeply from the waters of Christian demonology (see Frayling, 1996, p. 6). To take three influential, critically acclaimed, films dealing with the subject, Roman Polanski's *Rosemary's Baby* (1968), William Friedkin's *The Exorcist* (1973) and Richard Donner's *The Omen* (1976): all explicitly operate within the parameters of Western Christian demonology. Indeed, perhaps the most important of the above films, *Rosemary's Baby*, could almost be a filmic representation of the *Malleus*. Surprisingly, McGinn provides a very unperceptive review of the film, which simply fails to recognise the central themes of

---

[4] Also known as Henry Fuseli.

16

Western popular demonology. Although he is right to note that "... there is no overt reference to the Antichrist tradition" (McGinn, 1994, p. 272), there is certainly a strong implicit reference in the closing scene. Moreover, Polanski introduces us to a secretive group of individuals in the service of a personal Devil, to abominable satanic rites, to the suicide of a girl who had come into contact with such activity, to sexual intercourse between an incubus/Satan and the sedated Rosemary (Mia Farrow), and finally to the Genesis 6-like product of that union, the demon child.[5] More recently, should one be unfortunate enough to live in Sunnydale, the world view encouraged would not be wholly dissimilar to that of pre-modern Europe, in that, were it not for Buffy the Vampire Slayer, demons would swarm, obsess, possess and shape-shift at will (see Kaveney, 2001; Wilcox & Lavery, 2002). Indeed, there is even an episode, 'Gingerbread', that reflects contemporary satanic panics; only now, we are told, the demons actually do exist (see Tonkin, 2001, pp. 50-51). As J. Lawton Winslade (2002) explains:

> When two young children bearing occult symbols are found murdered, the usually oblivious town goes into uproar and suddenly we've entered the territory of media-frenzied incidents of "occult crimes". Even though we later learn the two children are manifestations of an ancient demon ... the episode is both amusing and chilling as the mothers of the town (the aptly titled MOO— Mothers Opposed to the Occult) turn on their own children and provoke a literal witch-hunt.

---

[5] Interestingly, Polanski appointed as his consultant for the film Anton LaVey, the founder, in 1966, of the Church of Satan and the author of several influential Satanist texts, most notably *The Satanic Bible* (1969).

If the concept of a unifying, personified source of evil still exists in Western Christian theology, the notion that there might also be swarming hordes of demons has, generally speaking, been abandoned. This, however, is not the case in popular culture and alien demonologies. Like the malevolent extraterrestrials of popular culture - the destructive, megalomaniac Martians of H. G. Wells's *The War of the Worlds* (1898) or, more recently, Tim Burton's *Mars Attacks!* (1996) and Roland Emmerich's *Independence Day* (1996) — they swarm like the hordes of hell. Alien demons are, like those that were cast out by Jesus, "legion" (Luke 8: 30). Again, unlike the alien messiah's of much theosophically-derived UFO religion, and very much like the demons of Christian history, screen aliens are a serious threat to human physical and spiritual well-being, and those who think otherwise are misguided and naïve. Indeed, *Mars Attacks!* bluntly ridicules the belief that aliens might be benevolent beings, with a concern for the environment and the spiritual welfare of humanity. Not only is the welcoming party, accompanied by starry-eyed "New Agers", quickly reduced to a scene of chaos and carnage by the visitors from space but, a few seconds after the dove of peace is poetically released from the hands of an enthusiastic idealist, it is swiftly reduced to smouldering, charred flesh by an alien ray gun.

The career of the demonic alien, however, was launched a century before *Mars Attacks!* H. G. Wells's Martians quickly captured the public imagination and went on to dominate popular culture.

> The influence and appeal of ... [*The War of the Worlds*] are apparent
>
> not only in its many editions and in the well-known effect of the
>
> radio play adaptation in 1938, but also in innumerable imitations

that have followed in the century since. As Arthur C. Clarke has written, the Menace from Space was virtually unknown before Wells but has become all too common since. (Dick, 1998, p. 112)

Although the alien messiah makes a brief appearance, particularly during the 1970s (see Ruppersberg, 1987), when "... a series of extremely popular science fiction movies ... featured extraterrestrials that are gentle, polite, wise, and above all, benevolent ... [possessing] a near saintly tolerance for human weakness and blundering" (Brain, 1983, p. 218), this was not to last. The basic premises of the alien messiah films were spectacularly overturned in 1979 by Ridley Scott's *Alien*. Standing in stark contrast to Steven Spielberg's *E.T.* (1982) and John Carpenter's slightly later *Starman* (1984), it mirrors emerging concerns about alien hostility; concerns which were fundamentally linked, in the 1970s, to stories of abductions. Beginning in the early 1970s, there was an exponential rise in reports of abductions (see Whitmore, 2000, p. 1), many of which included, like the accounts of demonic activity, "... copulation and general mischievous sexual encounters with aliens" (Bartholomew & Howard, 1998, p. 264), as well as horrific exploratory extraterrestrial surgery and viewing the disturbing results of reproductive experimentation, including alien–human hybrid babies. Like Rosemary's satanic baby and the children in *The Village of the Damned* (Rilla, Kinnoch, & Silliphant, 1960; Carpenter, Preger, King, & Himmelstein, 1995[6]), these hybrid infants are a threat. This is, for example, explained in chilling detail in the writings of David Jacobs (see Jacobs, 1998, p. 128-184). *Alien* powerfully reflects such

---

[6] Remade in 1995, *The Village of the Damned* is based on John Wyndham's *The Midwich Cuckoos.*

concerns about sexual interference and reproduction when a man is effectively raped by an extraterrestrial and later gives birth to the malign offspring through his chest. The demonised alien then quickly grows and becomes a predatory threat (as, like the *nephīlīm*, demons tend to). Again, in Norman J. Warren's obscure film, *Inseminoid* (1981), released as *Horrorplanet* in the USA, a woman is raped, becomes a cannibal, and gives birth to predatory, vampiric, alien twins. My point is that such alien offspring are essentially space *nephīlīm*, technological demons with appetites and habits reminiscent of their mythic forebears.

Although only attracting widespread fascination in the 1970s, this popular concern with alien abduction can be traced back to 1966, when John Lear published a series of articles on UFOs in the *Saturday Review* which brought to the public's attention the disturbing experiences of Barney and Betty Hill, who claimed that they had been abducted by aliens in 1961. This was followed by the publication of a book by Lear's co-editor at the *Saturday Review*, John Fuller. Fuller's widely read book, *The Interrupted Journey* (1966), together with a TV film of the same name, provided "... the model for the more sinister narratives which have come to dominate abduction literature" (Lavery, Hague, & Cartwright, 1996, p. 8; see also Matheson, 1998, pp. 47-76). That said, as Elaine Showalter has noted, it is likely that the Hills's experience "... incorporated imagery from a movie, *Invaders from Mars* [(Menzies, Alperson, Battle, & Blake, 1953)], and TV programs about space aliens" (Showalter, 1997, p. 191). That the malevolent aliens of science fiction found their way into the Hills's abduction story is interesting in that, over time, their own account generated a wave of interest that significantly contributed to the return of the malevolent alien in late 1970s popular culture; from which time it has become increasingly prominent, to the extent that it is now hard to imagine the screen alien as

20

anything other than malign. Indeed, the experiences reported by the Hills and narrative elements from *Invaders From Mars*, which include sexual interference, gynaecological testing, the taking of sperm samples, the placing of implants in the necks of humans, and subsequent changes in abductees' personalities, are all central to later portrayals of the alien in both popular culture and also abduction narratives (see, for example, Strieber, 1987, p. 30; Jacobs, 1998, p. 92).

Finally, it worth noting that, just as comparisons have been made with Western fairies and demons (Purkiss, 2000, pp. 15-17), so also comparisons have been made between the belief in fairies and alien abduction (Vallée, 1969; Purkiss, 2000, pp. 317-322). Not only are there a host of similarities between fairy lore and abduction narratives but, as Diane Purkiss argues:

> ... the similarities are most likely to be the result of common feelings. We might say that the fears and desires evoked and managed by such stories are so powerful that they have to have an outlet, and once fairies become too tame for such wild feelings, a new bogey has to be invented. We might add that fairies always came from an unknown that was both raw nature and vanished civilization — a rath in a wood, a graveyard. Now on earth there are no unknowns, no *terra incognita*. But there are still the stars. And there are no civilizations about which we know nothing except the silence of what they built. But beyond the solar system, who can know? The unknown is necessary for stories; its silence is what lets them be heard. In space, everyone can hear you scream. What alien stories do show - loud and clear - is that we need something to scream about.

21

However, that which gets us screaming the loudest is that which we fear the most. The alien which is simply an organic blob is laughable: e.g., *The Blob* (Yeaworth, Harris, Simonson, & Phillips, 1958; Russell, Harris, Harvey, & Darabont, 1988). The extraterrestrial which is unrecognisable green slime is derisory: e.g., *Inseminoid/Horrorplanet* (Warren, Gordon, Speechley, Maley, & Maley, 1981). But the malign personal being, which is amoral, humanoid, and demonic, carrying with it a history of diabolical baggage, is worth screaming about.

The malevolent alien in both popular culture and abduction narratives owes a great deal to the history of Christian demonology. The alien as technological demon is popular because it seems plausible; it seems plausible because it seems familiar; it seems familiar because it has been constructed from the myths and concepts of Western demonology.

Demonising the Extraterrestrial in Religious Discourse

Bearing in mind that the malevolent alien in both popular culture and abduction narratives owes much to the history of Christian demonology, it is perhaps unsurprising that those sections of the Christian community most vulnerable to satanic panics understand the extraterrestrial to be, quite literally, a demonic manifestation. As Ted Peters notes: "During the decade of the 1970s, numerous magazine articles and books appeared that dramatically challenged the alleged existence of UFOs and depicted the entire phenomenon as a Satanic plot" (Peters, 1995, pp. 197-198). As with the demonisation of elves in late Saxon England, extraterrestrials have been demonised in order to fit the good–evil dualism of the Christian world view. William Alnor, for example, makes the following statement:

22

I believe UFOs are real, but they represent a demonic delusion from the other side. I also believe that some of the flying vehicles they allegedly arrive in may be the work of fallen angels; they are not physical, but they are very real. (Alnor, 1998, p. 160)

Randall Baer insists that "... there is a profoundly potent force behind whatever the UFOs really are. That force is definitely demonic in nature and has extraordinary brainwashing effects on people" (Baer, 1989, p. 109). Again, Douglas Groothuis, operating with a similar hermeneutic of suspicion, writes: "Christians should reinterpret [extraterrestrials] as very possibly the malevolent masquerading of some very low demonic beings and monsters" (Groothuis, 1988, p. 31). Reflecting a key theme of Christian demonology, the purpose of these space demons is, says Frank Allnutt, "... to confuse people about the true source of salvation, the Lord Jesus Christ" (as cited in Peters, 1995, p. 199). That is to say, continuous with Christian demonology, the principal purpose of the extraterrestrial is to interfere spiritually with people by tempting them to look elsewhere for salvation, thereby disrupting their relationship with God.

This spiritualised Christian interpretation of the extraterrestrial as demon is literally inverted in certain new religious narratives: the spiritual demon is given physical form. Spiritual myths and concepts are understood in terms of physical, extraterrestrial realities. Hence, just as God and his angels are understood to be *benevolent* extraterrestrials so, in physicalist demonology, Satan and his devils are understood to be *malevolent* extraterrestrials. A good example of this interpretation is the following statement made in 1970 by Bob Geyer, the leader of the now defunct Church of Jesus the Saucerian:

> Satan, that old prince of darkness, and his legions of demons, are
> also beings from other worlds. They came down from another
> planet. Once, Satan was a member of God's astronauts. He became
> too greedy and too ambitious. He may have exploited the
> inhabitants of Earth, or other planets. He may have tricked people
> into slavery. (Geyer, as cited in Evans, 1984, p. 66)

Furthermore, complementing a broader soteriology, such demonologies function in much the same way as does Christian demonology. They constitute personifications of a good–evil dualism, in which humanity becomes embroiled. Benevolent extraterrestrials are now understood to protect humanity from malevolent extraterrestrials: "technological demons". Again, as in Christian demonology, such extraterrestrials are physically violent and sexually interested, but their primary concern, as the adversaries of goodness and truth, is to confound the plans the benevolent aliens have for humanity. Hence, again, whereas Jewish apocalyptic thought provided a spiritual interpretation of "… the clash of warring forces … in the earthly, political sphere" (Ling, 1968, p. 124), in UFO religion we see an inversion of that interpretation. The spiritual hosts and hordes are reconstituted as physical beings battling it out in the celestial sphere.

This dualism, although essentially Christian, is often very clearly articulated in groups which have their roots in the theosophical tradition. For example, as a member of the Aetherius Society told me: "We do acknowledge that there are malevolent forces outside the solar system. However, we are protected by benign cosmic intelligences who work ceaselessly on behalf of humanity". Similarly, this thesis is also developed by the Ashtar movement and Unarius, both of which have developed mythologies that betray the influence of Christian demonology. In her books *Project World Evacuation* (1982) and *Ashtar: A Tribute* (1985), Tuella (Thelma B. Terrill) explains that, although the space saviours are exercised over the build up of negative energy on the planet and the potentially catastrophic disruption of the Earth's magnetic field, they have also had to contend with the dark forces of other alien races. She presents "… detailed and complex information concerning the unfolding drama that she believed was playing out in the galaxy. Her work presented an epic narrative of battles between good and evil extraterrestrial forces" (Helland, 2003, p. 171), technological "principalities and powers" (cf. Ephesians 6: 12). Even more explicit in this respect is the narrative of *The Decline and Destruction of the Orion Empire* (1979), by Ruth Norman and the students of Unarius, which is essentially the story of the downfall of Satan, his opposition to the forces of good, and the subsequent fall of humanity, which now needs to be redeemed. The good–evil structure of the narrative has two key players: firstly, the co-founder of Unarius, Ruth Norman, known to her devotees as Uriel, "Archangel and Cosmic Visionary"; secondly, one of her students, known as Antares, who in a past life was "… the Fallen Angel, Satan, who had [in this life] come to [Uriel] to redeem himself" (Tumminia, 2003, p. 68). That said, although explicitly identified with Satan, in Unariun mythology he is known as Tyrantus, who, prior to his fall, was an advanced being on the planet Aries. Closely adhering to the Christian understanding of the origins of Satan, the narrative begins with a glorious angelic being whose pride leads him to challenge Uriel's authority and thereby to fall.

After many lifetimes Antares took on the body of Tyrantus, master of the galaxy and commander of doom. Tyrantus waged war on

25

other planets. According to Unariun belief, present-day students once resided in the Orion system. It was there they were enlisted to carry out evil deeds for Tyrantus. (Tumminia & Kirkpatrick, 1995, p. 94)

These evil deeds included opposition to, even torture of, Uriel for thousands of years. Hence, in this lifetime, through devotion to Uriel, they are seeking salvation by "working out their *karma*". However, the principal point as far as we are concerned is that, as Diana Tumminia notes: "Whether as Satan or Tyrantus ('the Terror of the Orion constellation'), in all the subsequent past life stories that emerged, Antares was cast as Uriel's evil foil" (Tumminia, 2003, p. 68).

This notion of the evil foil, of course, is useful in that it can be employed to explain failure. For example, the Ashtar movement explained a series of failed prophecies regarding alien intervention, as well as the proliferation of extraterrestrial messages which conflicted with the earlier communications of Ashtar, in terms of spiritual warfare. As Christopher Helland notes, "… messages and practices from a previous generation, which were thought not to be consistent with current cosmology and communications, were attributed to the interference of negative space beings in the upper atmosphere of the planet" (Helland, 2003, p. 174). This led to the development of a demonology in which "… several young members of Ashtar's training forces had defected and become evil beings." This, we are told:

… occurred decades ago when a group of cadets rebelled from the Ashtar Command and formed their own negative extraterrestrial government. These beings made alliances with "others of a similar rebellious nature" and began operating upon the "lowest planes closest to the Earth". Any messages that had been channelled in the past that contained overly negative information or erroneous dates for landing events were blamed upon these beings. (Helland, 2003, p. 174)

The significant point to note is that two groups with strong links to the theosophical tradition and its associated mythologies turn to the Christian tradition for their demonology. Indeed, as John Saliba has argued, the Unariun concept of God "... is somewhat vague and does not correspond to the Judeo-Christian idea of a personal, creator God" (Saliba, 2003, p. 195). As I have shown, this is not the case concerning Satan. The space gods may be theosophical, but the space demons are Christian. This is, I suggest, because Indian-influenced theosophy does not have a developed demonology that can easily be translated into physicalist religion. Whilst there are, of course, demonologies within the Indian religious tradition that could be used, such as that surrounding Māra (the adversary of Gautama Buddha), these are complex and not well-known (see Jayatilleke, 1975, pp. 256-258). Christian demonology, on the other hand, is, as I have argued, familiar and plausible.

To sum up thus far, we can identify perhaps five important areas of correspondence with Jewish apocalyptic and Christian demonology:

1. There is a cosmic battle between extraterrestrial principalities and powers.

2. There is a cosmic fall mythology to account for the existence of evil and the absence of love, peace, positive energy, etc. The once great being Antares fell, thereby

becoming Tyrantus, and members of Ashtar's training forces defected and became evil beings.

3. These "fallen" rebel forces are understood to be personified manifestations of evil, the adversaries and would-be usurpers of personified goodness. Hence, for example, the "negative extraterrestrial government" opposing Ashtar looks very much like an updated version of the demonic "... rulers of this present darkness ... the spiritual hosts of wickedness in heavenly places", which oppose God's government in the New Testament (Ephesians 6: 12). Moreover, the claim that these fallen beings exist on the "lowest planes closest to the Earth" comes very close to the Jewish apocalyptic belief noted above, that fallen angels hover in the lower air; a belief which subsequently fed into the Christian tradition and Western esotericism.

4. Spiritual problems, disagreements within the group, apostasy, and misinformation are manifestations of "demonic" interference.

5. Finally, the concept that "fallen" beings make alliances with "others of similar rebellious nature", overlaps with Western ideas concerning witchcraft and Faustian alliances. (We will see that the witch-craze, satanic panic, X-file-like belief that individuals make alliances with dark forces becomes explicit in some abduction demonologies.)

Another UFO group with roots in the theosophical subculture, but which has developed a far more explicit Christian demonology, is Heaven's Gate. Drawing very clearly on Christian apocalyptic thought, particularly as this is found in the Book of Revelation, the "exit statements" of members who later committed mass suicide make explicit reference to Christian demonology (see Partridge, 2006). We are told that there are "... forces against the Level Above Human", which "... distort any truth or reality of what the Kingdom of God is" (Chkody, 1999a), and that these are "... the 'Luciferian' forces in opposition to the Next Level" (Chkody, 1999a). Consequently, the founders of Heaven's Gate, Marshall Herff Applewhite and Bonnie Lu Nettles - also known as Ti and Do, Bo and Peep, and The Two - are given explicit space messiah status and their mission is understood in terms of opposition to demonic beings, referred to as the "space aliens" or "Luciferians". These demonic space aliens, we are told:

> ... are real and ... use what is termed as "UFOs". But their existence has carefully been made into legends or jokes to mask the reality of these physical beings. They have technology more advanced than that of humans, but behaviour that is no better. They have the same mammalian and egoistical behaviour that any human must learn to overcome ... These "space aliens" at one time ... were in training for service to the Next Level, but through weakness, aborted their opportunity to further their Next Level knowledge (*mind*) .... The agenda of these impostors is to distract and tempt those with deposits into their camp.... (Chkody, 1999b)

Western demonological ideas are conspicuous. Space aliens are fallen technological angels seeking to tempt humans away from the truth. Indeed, operating with a rigorous dualism, all the knowledge humans have is believed to "... come from two sources ... a) the Next Level - the Kingdom of God, or b) the opposition - the Lower Forces - Lucifer, Satan, or the Luciferians and their naïve servants" (Jnnody, 1999a).

As to the "deposits" mentioned in the above exit statement, these relate to what is in fact a theology of election in Heaven's Gate teaching, thereby betraying an essentially Reformed soteriology: which is perhaps not surprising considering that the founders' personal histories include involvement in Presbyterianism and the Baptist Church.[7] As with other UFO religions, the human race is believed to be the creation of superior extraterrestrials. Using a mixture of gardening and computing metaphors, it teaches that humans are beings with free will, placed in this "earthly garden" to grow spiritually. (There are other planetary gardens where other beings with free will grow.)

> [The] purpose of this creation is to produce new members for the Level Above Human..... New members of the Kingdom of Heaven are born through a metamorphic process which begins when the Level Above Human, or Next Level, "plants seeds" - places deposits or "chips" of Next Level mind (mind that comes from the Creator, the Chief of Chiefs, or Most High God - the term you use is not important) into human "plants".... A deposit is potentially the *gift of life*, for it contains the programming necessary to begin the metaphoric process which can lead to entry into the real Evolutionary Level Above Human, where there is no death. (Snnody, 1999)

Interestingly, this is similar to Justin's doctrine of the *spermatic logos*. Put simply, for Justin, reason (*logos*) unites God and humanity and makes possible the knowledge of God. Before the advent of Christ, Justin tells us, humans possessed seeds (*sperma*) of *logos* and thus were able to arrive at fragmentary truths about God. Hence, those who

---

[7] Applewhite, the son of a Presbyterian minister, had studied for the ministry and Nettles, although joining the Houston Theosophical Society later in life, was brought up a Baptist.

lived according to reason, such as the great philosophers, could be termed "Christians before Christ" (see Justin, in Stevenson, 1987, p. 61). (Christ, of course, was the *logos* made flesh.) However, unfortunately, there are demons which continually interfere with the divine-human relationship, tempting individuals away from reason, blinding them to the truth, and leading them to worship foreign gods. Heaven's Gate makes a very similar point:

> Although all religions contain seeds of truth which were planted by the Evolutionary Level Above Human, space aliens have twisted those truths so that souls might be blinded to the intended meaning and more easily influenced to do the opposite of what would be in their own interest. (Snnody, 1999)

Indeed, elsewhere, as in some streams of Christianity, a militantly exclusivist approach is taken to world faiths: " ... all religions have been spawned from the misinformation (distorted or corrupted truths) propagated by space-alien races ('Luciferians') who, knowingly or unknowingly, look to Lucifer as their god and victimize the humans on this planet" (Brnody, 1999).

This brings us explicitly to the doctrine of election. Extraterrestrials are understood to elect individuals and plant "deposits" in them. Such individuals are unaware of these deposits until they come into contact with a "Representative of the Level above Human", such as, particularly, Applewhite and Nettles. Moreover, just as the Christian elect respond to the preached gospel, so the deposit is only activated when it encounters a Next Level Mind. An activated deposit coincides with the joining of minds. That is to say, whereas the work of the Holy Spirit leads to the union and communion of the Christian with God which, in turn, involves a process of sanctification, in

31

Heaven's Gate teaching there is an activation of the deposit, a melding of the spiritually immature mind with the highly evolved mind, and a subsequent technological sanctification as the former mind is matured. However, the point for us to note is that Heaven's Gate understands Luciferians to be able to locate those with deposits and prevent them from graduating to the Next Level. Demons target the chosen and, again, tempt them away from faith in God and towards the pleasures of the world. Just as Satan tempted Christ in the wilderness (Matthew 4: 1-11), so, in Heaven's Gate demonology, the "Luciferians" tempt the elect with "mammalian behaviour" and the pleasures of this world. This has, in turn, led to a satanic panic mentality, which understands demonic forces to operate freely in the affairs of the secular world. Hence, the teaching and messages posted on the Heaven's Gate website are, like some Christian fundamentalist teaching, permeated with paranoia about sinister forces which control everything from the world's governments to shopping transactions. In many ways, the world for them is, as it was for Justin, "... swarming everywhere [with demons, which obsess] men's souls and bodies, infecting them with vice and corruption" (Kelly, 1977, p. 167; cf. Justin, in Stevenson, 1987, p. 60).

> We feel the current world economic systems are against all the guidelines given to humans by the Next Level at the beginning of and throughout this civilization. Although currency systems were not given to humans by the Next Level, we prefer to pay cash to using credit cards or purchase plans.... Banks are definitely tools of the "Luciferian" forces ... and we would prefer not to make any banking transactions ... [because] there are very real space-alien

forces in opposition to us who can use such things as bank accounts and mailing addresses against us. (Glnody, 1999)

Furthermore, it is believed that these Luciferian forces have particularly promoted sexual promiscuity in contemporary Western society. More specifically, and strongly suggestive of pre-modern Christian demonology, sexual desire *per se* is understood to be the result of demonic coercion: "The 'lower forces' have succeeded in totally addicting humans to mammalian behaviour. Everything from ads for toothpaste to clothing elevates human sexuality. Being from a genderless world, this behaviour is extremely hideous to us" (Glnody, 1999). The idea of being genderless and, particularly, celibate is, in common with certain streams of Christian thought, understood in terms of purity. Augustine, of course, understood sex negatively, it being fundamentally linked to the doctrine of original sin, the guilt of which was passed on by means of sexual intercourse. The following Heaven's Gate prayer (to Ti and Do!) illustrates this attitude to sexuality well[8]:

> I ask for your inner strength so that I may completely withdraw this vehicle from all the inner addictions of its animal flesh, and for your keenness so that I can block all thoughts or mental pictures of mammalian behaviour, and for your consistency in maintaining non-mammalian behaviour of the Evolutionary Level Above

---

[8] That said, whilst the link between the demonic and sex is developed along broadly Christian theological lines, its origin can perhaps be traced to Applewhite's guilt about his own double life, which vacillated between homosexual and heterosexual identities and a subsequent personally devastating dismissal from a university post after an affair with a student (see Balch, 1995, pp. 141-142).

Human - around the clock - in order that my soul (mind) will be compatible with and able to occupy a genderless vehicle from the Next Kingdom Level. (Brnody, 1999)

Division in the movement during the 1990s, following a general collapse of commitment, was, as we have seen it often is, interpreted in terms of demonic activity. During a period of research on the group, Robert Balch relates an episode that illustrates this well. Do and Ti had disappeared and the members were becoming demoralised. One member, Aaron, Balch recalls:

... received a "revelation" that split the group into factions. Aaron argued that the final step in the process of ridding ourselves of attachments was overcoming our dependence on The Two. Only by transcending our need for spiritual teachers could we be expected to enter the next kingdom. (Balch, 1995, p. 151)

In less than a week, three quarters of the group had adopted Aaron's thesis and defected. Word then came that The Two had "emerged from the wilderness" and that a big meeting was planned.[9] However, the rumour was unfounded; "Aaron re-emerged as a divisive force and factionalism increased". The point is that, in struggling to try and understand what was going on, the response was, as in the Ashtar movement, to turn to demonology. Hence, recalls Balch, "... some of the more committed members decided that our camp had been invaded by spirits. They laid the blame on a low-ranking Colorado recruit, claiming

---

[9] As was noted earlier with regard to the Jewish and Christian understandings of the desert/wilderness, much could be made of that statement in relation to demonology.

that he had been possessed by Beelzebub" (Balch, 1995, p. 152). Turning to the vulnerable in the group and accusing them of demonic activity is, as we have seen, not entirely without precedent in Western history.

It is important to note, however, that, as in Christian theology, regardless of the power of such dark forces, the demonised alien of UFO religion is never the superior of the benevolent, messianic alien. Consequently, with its roots firmly in the soil of Christian theology, Heaven's Gate is very clear that any plans the Next Level has will not ultimately be thwarted by Luciferian forces. This is developed with reference to the story in Genesis 3. Firstly, the following question is asked:

> Although the Lord knew that Lucifer was going to be in the garden and would use the forbidden fruit game to tempt Adam and Eve's resistance, didn't Adam have the opportunity to actually listen to the Lord as he gave those instructions, and not listen to other influences that came along (Luciferian)? (Jnnody, 1999b)

Secondly, they assume that their alien creators were aware of the presence of Luciferian forces. Thirdly, they insist on a doctrine of free will, which asserts that the original humans were in a position to follow freely either a Luciferian path or the Next Level path. Fourthly, they ask: "If this is so, could the Lord then have seen to it that the human kingdom would serve as a catalyst for humans to get out of what they shouldn't have gotten into in the first place?" (Jnnody, 1999b). Finally, they ask (and here the doctrine of election surfaces again): "Wouldn't this be especially true for those in whom the Lord takes an interest?" (Jnnody, 1999b). Hence, the argument is as follows:

35

a. God is able to rectify the situation and thereby overrule the Luciferian forces.

b. The process of returning to the Next Level is a process in which, as in some Christian theologies,[10] "the Luciferians unknowingly serve the Level Above Human by being a catalyst for growth" (Snnody, 1999).

c. In accord with Christian eschatology, the demonic forces know that they will finally be defeated at the end of the age: "They are for the most part aware that with the cyclical spading-under of the garden, which is imminent as this is the end of the age, their ranks are scheduled to be recycled as well" (Snnody, 1999).

The Reptilian Agenda

Having looked at UFO religion, I now want to focus on a new breed of demonic alien evolving within contemporary "abduction spiritualities",[11] which almost certainly has its origins in popular culture: especially the popular fantasy magazine *Weird Tales*. H. P. Lovecraft, Clarke Ashton Smith and, particularly, Robert E. Howard wrote stories for

---

[10] Donald Bloesch expresses the position well: "The Bible posits a moral but not a metaphysical dualism, for biblical faith is adamant that the devil and his hosts are both restrained and used by the living God, to whom alone belongs ultimate power.... [Although] evil is not directly willed by God, it is under his controlling power. Behind the afflictions and sufferings of the human race lies the malevolent work of Satan, and behind his abysmal power lies the inscrutable hand of the living God.... He governs humanity both through the devil and cruel tyrants on the one hand and through just rulers on the other" (1995, pp. 129-130). This, of course, removes any ultimate dualism but, as the apocalyptic writers were aware, in so doing brings culpability for ultimate evil uncomfortably close to God.

[11] I distinguish UFO religion from abduction spirituality as follows: unlike the former, the latter is (a) usually held or taught by an individual, rather than an organised group or church; and (b) the result of, and/or focuses on, claimed experiences of alien abduction.

Weird Tales which included malign, subterranean serpent creatures. In one of Howard's stories, "The Shadow Kingdom" (1929/1976), they were able to change into human form in order to insinuate themselves into positions of power in human society (see Barkun, 2003, p. 121). This theme is then developed by other writers and conspiracy theorists who produce "fact-fiction reversals" (Barkun, pp. 29-33), or accounts which significantly blur the distinction between fact and fiction. Of particular note is Maurice Doreal, who had been involved in the theosophical subculture and subsequently founded the Brotherhood of the White Temple (ca. 1930). Doreal developed elaborate theories about a subterranean serpent race and, subsequently, incorporated extraterrestrials into his thinking in the early 1950s. These themes were later elided in order to produce a theory of a serpent race which, he claimed, would become in the latter half of the twentieth century an ally of the Antichrist (Doreal, ca. 1964, pp. 29, 47-50; Barkun, p. 119). Although we need not explore the "inner-earth" conspiracies associated with serpent creatures, it is worth remembering that, as Michael Barkun comments, in the popular imagination the subterranean world "... is the location of hell, where the devil supervises the punishments endured by the wicked. And Satan, the Evil One, is also the serpent who deceived Eve in the Garden of Eden, bringing humanity sin and mortality" (Barkun, p. 123). Hence, that these reptile beings originally reside in a subterranean underworld is significant. At this early stage, we see:

a. A reptilian creature step out of the pages of fiction into the occult subculture.

b. The elision of the reptile with popular UFO lore of the early 1950s.

c. An explicit relationship being established with Christian demonology.

In contemporary UFO demonologies, these creatures, often referred to as "reptilians" or "reptoids" and, less frequently, "insectoids" (e.g. Jacobs, 1998, p. 94), are usually described as a "... tall, mostly humanoid-type race, with snake-like eyes and skin" (Icke, 2001, p. xxi). Tony Dodd, a British UFO researcher, describes "... a seven-foot-tall lizard, only with arms and legs", which is aggressive and highly intelligent (Dodd, 1999, pp. 203, 232). Whilst the greys - the slim aliens with large, dark, almond-shaped eyes - are sometimes understood to be malevolent (in that they experiment on humans), it is the reptilians and reptoids that are beginning to dominate contemporary extraterrestrial demonology. Gail Seymour, a contactee and psychic healer specialising in the treatment of abductees, claims that they rape, torture and murder. She recounts how she first became aware of the reptilians: "About six months ago I noticed that all of my new clients were being raped and tortured by an 'unseen force' - a force that was definitely not the greys". As to why this species of alien is suddenly becoming prominent: since mid-August 1999, according to Seymour (she is very specific about the pre-millennium timing) "... there has been a change of command. The greys, formerly intermediaries for the reptilians, acting as their front line of attack, seem to have stepped backward. The reptilians are now coming forward" (Seymour, 2002a).

Not only has popular fiction apparently become fact, but also the parallels with pre-modern accounts of incubi and succubi are often conspicuous. Indeed, there is clearly a sense in which reptilians are understood to be a spiritual threat. Some victims, for example, speak of "possession" and, according to one, "... a sucking effect in [the] solar plexus 'like a vacuum cleaner'" (Seymour, 2002a). Indeed, as we have seen in Doreal's thought, Christian demonology is explicitly used. For example, according to

Seymour (2002b): "Satan was real alright. I think he was a big deal and the head of the reptilian invasion... ". Again, reptilian demonologies make much of the biblical account of the serpent tempting Eve, which, we are told, was actually the initial reptilian contact with humans.

Almost certainly because it provides a physicalist account of Christian demonology, the popularity of the reptilian has spread more within abduction narratives than within UFO groups *per se*. The demon interferes directly with the human. Consequently, the increase in reports about reptilians follows the increased interest in abduction generally. Parallel to the shift in popular culture, which was in turn linked to the rise of interest in abduction, reptilian demonologies are becoming far more common. Even Michelle LaVigne's otherwise very positive interpretation of extraterrestrials, *The Alien Abduction Survival Guide*, reports the following discussion with Hetar, a beneficent alien with whom she has developed a relationship: "Hetar once showed a picture of an ET that looked like a humanoid/lobster/lizard mix. He told me to be careful of these ETs. I asked why. He said, 'Because they will eat you'" (LaVigne, 1995, p. 83). Similarly, reptilians have begun to find their way into the theologically positive theosophical streams of the Ashtar Command. For example, on the website of the Ashtar Lightwork Center, where it is difficult to find anything negative about extraterrestrials, we read the following testimony (by one who, significantly, was clearly aware of abduction demonologies):

My first conscious contact with a so-called Alien in this life was with one of the people commonly referred to as Greys.... One night when my sister Galimai-A and myself were in the living room, talking, a silver-gray coloured lady stood at the entrance, and asked politely if she could please come in. She spoke telepathically.... Of course I first was a bit suspicious. I also knew of the nasty abduction stories.... But she insisted she was not of that part of the race.... She told us the "bad guys" are not silvery gray, like herself and her benign people, but a dullish brownish gray, [because] all the spiritual light had gone from them. This part of the race chose a connection to the Reptilians. They have cut themselves off from the light ... affiliated with the reptilians ... [and] live on another planet, where they are closely guarded by the Ashtar Command (Ashtar Light Network, 2003).

The text goes on to relate how some aliens fell by allying themselves with the reptilians and "... functioning like the Borg in *Star Trek*". The result was a great battle between good and evil aliens: the visitor "... showed us some of the things that happened during that war", things that "... were ten times worse than Roddenberry was allowed to show" (Ashtar Light Network, 2003). This last point both indicates Christian influence and also suggests that *Star Trek* is understood to have been used by extraterrestrials to reveal truth.

This myth of an ancient battle between good and evil aliens, the result of which is the dominance of the reptilians, is particularly developed in the surreal conspiracy theories of David Icke. Indeed, Icke is perhaps most responsible for developing and popularising the demonology. This is particularly interesting, since his ideas can be traced back very clearly to Doreal (and thus to Robert Howard's fiction). For example, Doreal produced a long poem, "The Emerald Tablets" (ca. 1930/2002), which, he claimed, was the work of Thoth, a priest who had lived in Atlantis. This text is important, not only because it mentions demonic serpent creatures, but also because it is used extensively by David Icke (see, particularly, Icke, 2001). Indeed, many of Doreal's themes are explicit in Icke's work.

In recent years, Icke has devoted his career to exposing "the reptilian agenda", the ultimate aim of which is the "… control of planet Earth and its entire population". Icke's conspiracy theory, which Seymour told me she shared,[12] includes the belief that the world's leaders, including US Presidents, the British royal family, and even leading religious figures, belong to a shape-shifting, reptilian–human hybrid bloodline (see Icke, 1999). This is perhaps the most recent manifestation of another conspiracy theory, one which concerns a group of malevolent individuals, collectively referred to as the Illuminati (see Barkun, 2003, pp. 45-64). The original thesis can be traced back to John Robison, a Professor of Natural Philosophy at the University of Edinburgh, who published a work in 1797 claiming to expose "… a conspiracy against all the religions and governments of Europe" (Robison, 1797/1967). His book included a discussion of the Bavarian intellectual Adam Weishaupt, who sought to propagate Enlightenment thought through a secretive society, which he founded in 1776, called the Order of the Illuminati. Although Weishaupt was removed from his post as Professor of Canon Law at the University of Ingolstadt and his Order suppressed, Robison and others were convinced that the Illuminati, as well as the Freemasons and other secret societies, continued to spread their influence in an effort to secure world domination. Because secret societies, such as, particularly, the Freemasons, were already suspected of conspiring with the

---

[12] I have been surprised at the number of those I have spoken to who find Icke's ideas, if not entirely convincing, at least plausible.

Devil, the thesis seemed plausible to many. Over time, the confluence of conspiracist ideas led to the construction of a metanarrative which claimed that:

> ... individual Masons influenced by the Order of the Illuminati were in league with the Devil (as agents of the Antichrist) - a claim that quickly became entwined with allegations that Jews were behind the plot. These claims of conspiracy made their way to the United States in the 1800s, generating Protestant suspicion about Freemasons and Catholics. (Berlet, 2001, p. 231)

The Illuminati conspiracy has proved to be enormously popular over the last 200 years (see Barkun, 2003, pp. 45-64). Although today's conspiracy theorists may be unaware of Robison or Weishaupt, in my own conversations with people I have been surprised at how often the conspiracy surfaces. I have come across several variations of it in the last few years, most of which link the Illuminati to what the geographer Richard Peet has referred to as the "unholy trinity": the International Monetary Fund, the World Bank and the World Trade Organization (Peet, et al., 2003).[13] Indeed, it is arguable that Icke's own development of the Illuminati conspiracy, which is linked to such dominant global institutions, accounts, to some extent, for his

---

[13] Richard Peet and his co-authors are not conspiracy theorists and their interesting book on neo-liberalism is not concerned with such theories. However, the point is that the cogent thesis of the book (and other treatments of the "unholy trinity") could easily be interpreted in this way. Add a sentence about the Illuminati to the following statement printed on the cover and it comes very close to David Icke's theories and those of other conspiracy theorists: "The lives of all of us, particularly if we live in developing countries, are intimately affected by a triad of hugely powerful, well-financed, but fundamentally undemocratic and out of control organizations - the International Monetary Fund, the World Bank and the World Trade Organization".

growing popularity. For example, some people I have spoken to disagree with the reptilian component of his thesis, but genuinely think that his overall conspiracist understanding of history and world affairs is fundamentally correct.

Icke's relatively complex thesis is interesting in that, whilst it is highly critical of Christianity, its fundamental ideas demonstrate a dependence on Christian demonology. This becomes explicit when he traces the origins of the reptilian occupation of Earth. Although Icke had been developing his conspiracy theories for several years (see Icke, 1994), and although an interest in UFOs is evident in his earlier books, in the second half of the 1990s his emphasis shifted very firmly towards an extraterrestrial demonology. Following popular writers such as Erich von Däniken (1969) and Zecharia Sitchin (1990), and in a similar way to the Raëlian Church and Heaven's Gate, he provides a physicalist reinterpretation of the Genesis accounts of encounters between supernatural beings and humans (see Partridge, 2003, pp. 21-26). However, unlike much UFO religion, the consequences of this alien–human contact for Icke are almost entirely negative: "The Old Testament", he notes, "talks about the 'Sons of God' who interbred with the daughters of men to create the hybrid race, the Nefilim [sic]" (Icke, 2003b). It is these hybrid beings that constitute Icke's reptilian demonology. Again, following Sitchin, he claims that: "Sumerian clay tablets ... talk of a race of 'gods' from another world who brought advanced knowledge to the planet and interbred with humans to create hybrid bloodlines" (Icke, 2003b). Turning to mythological civilisations, he argues that

... way back in 'pre-history', there was a highly developed civilization in the Pacific, which has become known as Lemuria, or

43

Mu. These peoples and others also founded another great civilization on a landmass in the Atlantic, which we know as Atlantis. (Icke, 2001, p. xxi)

Betraying some chronological snobbery, his point is that aliens can be traced throughout the ancient and mythical civilisations by simply linking them to great architectural and engineering achievements. In other words, he assumes that our ancient forebears were incapable of such work and insists that "... the knowledge that built fantastic and unexplainable ancient structures like the Great Pyramid and other amazing sites across the world" was extraterrestrial; they were all constructed by "extraterrestrials of many varieties" (Icke, 2001, p. xxi). However, at this early period, good and evil alien races co-existed on Earth. This led to tensions and battles for supremacy. Alien races engaged in warfare until alliances were made as a result of interbreeding. Of particular significance was the interbreeding between the reptilians and "the blond-haired, blue-eyed Nordic peoples" (Icke, 2001, p. xxi), the outcome of which was the ancient Aryan "master race". Subsequently, according to Icke, "... these hybrid bloodlines ... were put into the positions of ruling power, especially in the ancient Near and Middle East, in advanced cultures like Sumer, Babylon, and Egypt" (Icke, 2001, p. xxi). Hence, he believes that he has identified, not only a fundamental demonic continuity between Aryanism and Nazism, but also hybrid reptilian bloodlines, which can be traced through history. It is these bloodlines that "... later became the royal and aristocratic families of Europe". Moreover, he says:

... thanks to the ... British Empire and other European empires, they were exported to the Americas, Australia, New Zealand, and right across into the Far East, where they connected with other reptilian hybrid bloodlines, like those, most obviously in China, where the symbolism of the dragon is the very basis of their culture. (Icke, 2003b)

Hence, the "biggest secret" as he calls it (Icke, 1999), is that:

... a global secret society called the Illuminati ... have (sic) been holding the reigns of power in the world since ancient times.... The Illuminati have been working to a long planned and coordinated agenda to create a world government, central bank, army, and a micro-chipped population linked to a global computer. (Icke, 2003c)

Concerning the Illuminati, Icke is again explicitly indebted to a mixture of ideas drawn from popular conspiracy theory and Christian demonology, in that he understands them to be practising Satanists (see Icke, 2001, pp. 312-334). However, as with Seymour, and unlike conspiracy theorists who stand explicitly within the Christian tradition (as Robison did), the term "satanic" is essentially synonymous with "reptilian". "Satanists" are those who are committed to the demonic reptilian agenda and the reptilians themselves are involved in all the activities popularly attributed to Satan and Satanism. He says that:

My use of the term Satanism ... [describes] a system of ritual sacrifice and torture which, staggering as it may seem to most people, is commonplace all over the world today. Satanism is another name for the worship of a highly destructive, negative force which has been given endless names over the centuries. Nimrod,

45

Baal, Moloch or Molech, Set, the Devil, Lucifer, there is no end to them. (Icke, 2003d)

Hence, in words strikingly similar to some Christian fundamentalist statements about Satanists, reptilian–human hybrids are continually and systematically involved in "... the abuse and satanic ritual abuse of children, and human sacrifice ceremonies in general" (Icke, 2003b). He continues:

> ... follow the Illuminati-reptilian bloodlines from the ancient world to now and they have ALWAYS taken part in human sacrifice ceremonies and blood-drinking. The sacrifices to "the gods" in ancient accounts were literally sacrifices to the reptilians and their hybrid bloodlines. The story of the blood-drinking Dracula is symbolic of the reptilian "vampires". (Icke, 2003b)

As to why the vampiric reptilians need to drink human blood, the answer is simple. If they do not, they are unable to "... maintain their DNA codes in their 'human' expression" (Icke, 2003b). In other words, without blood, "... they manifest their reptilian codes and we would all see what they really look like" (Icke, 2003b). This is why, declares Icke, "... people like George Bush, Henry Kissinger, and a stream of the other Illuminati 'big names'" need to be exposed "... as reptilian shape-shifters who take part in human sacrifice and blood drinking. The two go together" (Icke, 2003b).

Icke not only offers people an extraterrestrial version of satanic panic demonology, but a version which is fundamentally rooted in and dependent upon that demonology. Indeed, just as those involved in witch crazes and satanic panics become paranoid and obsessed

46

with conspiracy theories, convinced that the servants of Satan operate all around them - the priest, the teacher, the doctor, the social worker, the shop assistant, the police officer or indeed anyone who acts out of the ordinary - so, understanding reality to be multidimensional, Icke argues that reptilians live, unseen, all around us in a fourth dimension. This dimension is significant, he says, because it is "... the traditional home for the 'demons' of folklore and myth" (Icke, 2003a). Again, just as demons are able to work through their human accomplices in witch craze and satanic panic cosmologies, so, in Icke's thought, "... fourth-dimensional reptilian entities work through hybrid bloodlines because [being part reptilian] they have a vibrational compatibility with each other" (Icke, 2003a).

This mythology is, as noted above, reinforced through popular culture. However, in Icke's case, this reinforcement is not passive, but active. That is to say, Icke urges those new to his ideas to study, for example, Kenneth Johnson's TV series *V* (NBC, 1984-1985), which, he claims, will educate people about "what is REALLY going on" (Icke, 2003b). Indeed, the overlap between the basic structure of Icke's demonology and the storyline of *V* is so striking that it is hard to avoid the conclusion that it has been a significant factor in its construction: particularly bearing in mind that it was written before Icke produced his own demonology. Essentially, *V* is about reptilian extraterrestrials which, whilst appearing respectable and friendly, are actually a malevolent, vampiric species who eat humans and plot to take over the planet. Other films he explicitly endorses include *The Matrix* (Wachowski, Wachowski, & Silver, 1999), which is clearly viewed by him as an important exposé (Icke, 2001, p. xvii), John Carpenter's *They Live* (1988), which tells the story of a drifter who accidentally uncovers an alien plot to take over America, and David Schmoeller's *The Arrival* (1990), in

47

which an alien parasite turns a human into a vampire. "I urge you", he says, "to think about watching these movies to get up to speed if you are new to all of this" (Icke, 2003b).

Icke, of course, is not alone in claiming that aliens actively use popular culture to educate us. For example, in a channelled message from Soltec of the Ashtar Command, we are given the following information:

> We will enter into a campaign of spreading our imagery through your media…. So-called fictional sci-fi books, which will gain mass popularity, will actually be truth disguised as fiction. This will gently accustom humans to the concept of the Ashtar Command…. Your media culture is the strongest influence on your Western society and it is therefore obvious that we would begin to announce ourselves to the mass consciousness in this manner. (Soltec, 2003).

Conclusion

The thesis of this lecture is that, while much UFO religion has its roots in theosophical thought, its demonology is firmly rooted in the Christian tradition. Whilst the extraterrestrial saviours are theosophical (Partridge, 2003, pp. 7-21), and whilst doctrines of reincarnation and *karma* are often employed, when it comes to the construction of a demonology, UFO religionists, contactees and abductees quite naturally turn to the myths and ideas with which they are most familiar. Consequently, alien demonologies function in much the same way as popular Christian demonologies and, in extreme cases, tend to inspire responses similar to those evident in the witch craze, in the conspiracy theories of the eighteenth and nineteenth centuries, and the more recent satanic panics. Indeed, even strongly theosophical groups that deny the existence of an actual Devil or any form of ontological evil still seem bound to the conceptual framework of Jewish apocalyptic and Christian demonologies. For example, whereas Mark-Age states that "... there is no such thing as a Satan", Christian terminology and mythology is nevertheless used. Satan is simply reinterpreted as "... the evil that lives in men's minds, hearts, desires, ambitions and greed" (Mark-Age, 2003). This, moreover, is the Satan of the New Testament that tempted Christ. Hence, whereas in the more traditional theosophical narratives there is a tendency to internalise the demonic, this detraditionalised demonology is still fundamentally Christian, in that many of the same themes are discussed, including the temptation away from the plan of the Creator and the celestial battle of Armageddon,[14] information about which is channelled by the archangel Michael, and the effects of which are manifest in the wars, disasters and sufferings of human history.

The external demon, we have seen, has been particularly promoted by abduction narratives and conspiracy theories, both of which are most obviously evident in "the reptilian agenda". Being far more dependent on external malign entities, they have drawn explicitly on biblical and popular Christian demonologies.

Finally, along with Christian demonology, the demonised alien is principally shaped by popular culture. That said, we have seen that this too has been informed by a demonology that runs like a continuous thread from Jewish apocalypticism to the reptilian agenda. Indeed, I

---

[14] Armageddon is detraditionalised in that it seems to be the battle to transform corrupt human selves: "We have come to the place in the Battle of Armageddon where each person must accept responsibility for the conditions prevailing everywhere on the planet" (Mark-Age, 2003).

would be unsurprised to learn that many new Western demonologies outside UFO religion are also fundamentally Christian.

References

Adamski, G. (1949). *Pioneers of space: A trip to the moon, Mars and Venus.* Los Angeles: Leonard-Freefield.

Alnor, W. M. (1998). *UFO cults and the new millennium.* Grand Rapids, MI: Baker Books.

Ashtar Lightwork Center. (2003). *The Greys (Zetas) - unbiased.* Retrieved January 9, 2003, from: http://www.ashtarlightworkcenter.com/greys/index. htm.

Augustine, Saint. (1945). *The city of God* (J. Healey, Trans.). London: J. M. Dent. (Original work written ca. 413-426).

Baer, R. N. (1989). *Inside the New Age nightmare: A former New Age leader takes you on a dramatic journey.* Lafayette, LA: Huntington House.

Bailey, M. D. (2003). *Battling demons: Witchcraft, heresy, and reform in the late Middle Ages.* University Park, PA: Pennsylvania State University Press.

Baker, A. (2000). *The encyclopaedia of alien encounters.* London: Virgin.

Balch, R. W. (2000). Waiting for the ships: Disillusionment and the revitalization of faith in Bo and Peep's UFO cult. In J. R. Lewis (Ed.), *UFOs and popular culture: An encyclopaedia of contemporary myth* (pp. 137-166). Santa Barbara, CA: ABC-Clio.

Barkun, M. (2003). *A culture of conspiracy: Apocalyptic visions in contemporary America.* Berkeley, CA: University of California Press.

Bartholomew, R. E., & Howard, G. S. (1998). *UFOs & alien contact: Two centuries of mystery.* Amherst, NY: Prometheus Books.

Berlet, C. (2001). The Illuminati. In B. E. Brasher (Ed.), *Encyclopedia of fundamentalism* (pp. 231-232). New York: Routledge.

Blavatsky, H. P. (1877). *Isis unveiled: A master-key to the mysteries of ancient and modern science and theology.* (2 vols.). New York: J. W. Bouton.

Blavatsky, H. P. (1888). *The secret doctrine: The synthesis of science, religion and philosophy.* (2 vols.). London: Theosophical Publishing Company.

Bloesch, D. G. (1995). *God the Almighty: Power, wisdom, holiness, love.* Carlisle: Paternoster Press.

Bolt, P. G. (1996). Jesus, the daimons and the dead. In A. N. S. Lane (Ed.), *The unseen world: Christian reflections on angels, demons and the heavenly realm* (pp. 75-102). Carlisle: Paternoster Press.

Bonhoeffer, D. (1955). *Temptation* (K. Downham, Trans.). London: SCM Press. (Original work published 1953).

Bowie, F. (2000). *The anthropology of religion: An introduction.* Oxford: Blackwell.

Brain, B. (1983). Saviors and scientists: Extraterrestrials in recent science fiction films. *Et Cetera: A Review of General Semantics, 40* (2), 218-229.

Briggs, R. (1996). *Witches & neighbours: The social and cultural context of European witchcraft.* London: HarperCollins.

Brnody. (1999). *Up the chain.* Retrieved August 26, 1999, from:

http://www.heavensgatetoo.com/exitchk.htm.

Burton, T. (Director/Producer), Franco, L. J. (Producer), & Gems, J. (Writer). (1996). *Mars attacks!* [Motion picture]. United States: Warner Bros.

Carpenter, J. (Director), Franco, L. J. (Producer), & Evans, B. A., & Gideon, R. (Writers). (1984). *Starman* [Motion picture]. United States: Columbia Pictures.

Carpenter, J. (Director), Preger, M., & King, S. (Producers), & Himmelstein, D. (Writer). (1995). *Village of the damned* [Motion picture]. United States: Universal Pictures.

Carpenter, J. (Writer/Director), & Franco, L. J. (Producer). (1988). *They live* [Motion picture]. United States: Alive Films (Universal Studios [Distributor]).

Chkody. (1999a). *Earth exit statement.* Retrieved August 26, 1999, from:

http://www.heavensgatetoo.com/exitchk.htm.

Chkody. (1999b). *The hidden facts of Ti and Do.* Retrieved August 26, 1999, from:

http://www.heavensgatetoo.com/exitchk.htm.

Clines, D. (1996). The significance of the "sons of God" episode (Genesis 6: 1-4) in the context of the "primeval history" (Genesis 1-11). In J. W. Rogerson (Ed.), *The Pentateuch: A Sheffield reader* (pp. 33-46). Sheffield: Sheffield Academic Press.

Däniken, E. von (1969). *Chariots of the gods?: Unsolved mysteries of the past* (M. Heron, Trans.). London: Souvenir Press. (Original work published 1968).

Dick, S. J. (1998). *Life on other worlds: The 20th century extraterrestrial life debate.* Cambridge: Cambridge University Press.

Dodd, T. (1999). *Alien investigator: The case files of Britain's leading UFO detective.* London: Headline.

Donner, R. (Director), Bernhard, H. (Producer), & Seltzer, D. (Writer). (1976). *The omen* [Motion picture]. United States: Twentieth Century-Fox Film Corporation.

Doreal, M. (ca. 1964). *Flying saucers: An occult viewpoint.* Sedalia, CO: Brotherhood of the White Temple.

Doreal, M. (2002). *The emerald tablets of Thoth-the-Atlantean: A literal translation of one of the most ancient and secret of the great works of the ancient wisdom* (M. Doreal, Trans.); Together with *An interpretation of the emerald tablets,* by Dr Doreal. Sedalia, CO: Brotherhood of the White Temple. (Original work published ca. 1930).

Emmerich, R. (Writer/Director), & Devlin, D. (Writer/Producer). (1996). *Independence day* [Motion picture]. United States: Twentieth Century-Fox Film Corporation.

Evans, H. (1984). Demonic UFOs. In P. Brookesmith (Ed.), *UFOs: Where do they come from?: Contemporary theories on the origin of the phenomenon* (pp. 62-74). London: Orbis.

Festinger, L., Riecken, H. W., & Schachter, S. (1964). *When prophecy fails: A social and psychological study of a modern group that predicted the end of the world.* New York: Harper & Row. (Original work published 1956).

Forsyth, N. (1987). *The old enemy: Satan and the combat myth.* Princeton, NJ: Princeton University Press.

Frayling, C. (1996). *Nightmare: The birth of horror.* London: BBC.

Friedkin, W. (Director), & Blatty, W. P. (Writer/Producer). (1973). *The exorcist* [Motion picture]. United States: Warner Bros.

Fuller, J. G. (1966). *The interrupted journey: Two lost hours aboard a flying saucer.* New York: Dial Press.

Galloway, A. D. (1951). *The cosmic Christ.* London: Nisbet.

Glnody (1999). *Why we must leave at this time.* Retrieved August 26, 1999, from:

http://www.heavensgatetoo.com/exitchk.htm.

Groothuis, D. R. (1988). *Confronting the New Age: How to resist a growing religious movement.* Downers Grove, IL: InterVarsity Press.

Hall, S. G. (1991). *Doctrine and practice in the early Church.* London: SPCK.

Helland, C. (2003). From extraterrestrials to ultraterrestrials: The evolution of the concept of Ashtar.

In C. Partridge (Ed.), *UFO religions* (pp. 162-178). London: Routledge.

Howard, R. E. (1976). *The shadow kingdom, and others.* St. Albans: Panther. ("The shadow kingdom" originally published in *Weird Tales*, August, 1929).

Icke, D. (1994). *The robots' rebellion: The story of the spiritual renaissance.* Bath: Gateway.

Icke, D. (1999). *The biggest secret.* Scottsdale, AZ: Bridge of Love Publications.

Icke, D. (2001). *Children of the matrix: How an interdimensional race has controlled the world for thousands of years: And still does.* Scottsdale, AZ: Bridge of Love Publications.

Icke, D. (2003a). *A concise description of the Illuminati.* Retrieved January 6, 2003, from: http://www.davidicke.com/icke/articles/illuminati.html.

Icke, D. (2003b). *The reptilian connection.* Retrieved January 6, 2003, from: http://www.davidicke.com/icke/temp/reptconn.html

Icke, D. (2003c). *Who really rules the world?* Retrieved January 6, 2003, from:

http://www.davidicke.com/icke/visitor.html.

Icke, D. (2003d). *Who are the draconians?: Case files of Branton: Case file #32.* Retrieved January 6, 2006, from: http://reptile.users2.50megs.com/research/r100799c.html.

Jacobs, D. M. (1998). *The threat: The secret alien agenda.* London: Simon & Schuster.

Jayatilleke, K. N. (1975). *The message of the Buddha.* London: Allen and Unwin.

Jnnody. (1999a). *Incarnating and discarnating.* Retrieved August 26, 1999, from: http://www.heavensgatetoo.com/exitchk.htm.

Jnnody. (1999b). *Be fruitful and multiply.* Retrieved August 26, 1999, from: http://www.heavensgatetoo.com/exitchk.htm.

Johnson, K. (Writer/Director). (1983-1985). *V* [Television series]. New York: NBC.

Jolly, K. L. (1996). *Popular religion in late Saxon England: Elf charms in context.* Chapel Hill, NC: University of North Carolina Press.

Jones, P., & Pennick, N. (1995). *A history of pagan Europe.* London: Routledge.

Jung, C. G. (1969). *Flying saucers: A modern myth of things seen in the skies* (R. F. C. Hull, Trans.). New York: Signet Books. (Original work published 1958).

Kaveney, R. (Ed.). (2001). *Reading the Vampire Slayer: The unofficial critical companion to Buffy and Angel.* London: Tauris Parke.

Kelly, J. N. D. (1977). *Early Christian doctrines.* (5th ed.). London: A. and C. Black. (Original work published 1958).

King, G. R. (1934). *Unveiled mysteries.* Chicago: Saint Germain Press.

Kluger, R. S. (1967). *Satan in the Old Testament* (H. Nagel, Trans.). Evanston, IL: Northwestern University Press. (Original work published 1948).

La Fontaine, J. (1999). Satanism and satanic mythology. In B. Ankarloo & S. Clark (Eds.), *Witchcraft and magic in Europe: The twentieth century* (pp. 81-140). Philadelphia: University of Pennsylvania Press.

Lagrange, P. (2000). Kenneth Arnold. In J. R. Lewis (Ed.), *UFOs and popular culture: An encyclopaedia of contemporary myth* (p. 34). Santa Barbara, CA: ABC-Clio.

Lavery, D., Hague, A., & Cartwright, M. (1996). Introduction: Generation X - the X-files and the cultural moment. In D. Lavery, A. Hague, & M. Cartwright, (Eds.), *"Deny all knowledge": Reading the X-files* (pp. 1-21). London: Faber and Faber.

LaVey, A. S. (1969). *The satanic Bible.* New York: Avon Books.

LaVigne, M. (1995). *The alien abduction survival guide: How to cope with your ET experience.* Newberg, OR: Wild Flower Press.

Leadbeater, C. (1912). *A textbook of theosophy.* Adyar: Theosophical Publishing House.

Ling, T. (1961). *The significance of Satan: New Testament demonology and its contemporary relevance.* London: SPCK.

Ling, T. (1968). *A history of religion, East and West: An introduction and interpretation.* London: Macmillan.

Luther, M. (1960). *Luther's works, vol. 2: Lectures on Genesis: Chapters 6-14* (J. Pelikan, Ed.; D. E. Poellot, Ass. Ed.; G. V. Schick, Trans.). St. Louis, MO: Concordia Publishing House. (Original work published 1543).

Mark-Age. (2003). *I am nation newsletter.* Retrieved January 7, 2003, from:

http://www.islandnet.com/~arton/markage.html.

Matheson, T. (1998). *Alien abductions: Creating a modern phenomenon.* Amherst, NY: Prometheus Books.

McGinn, B. (1994). *Antichrist: Two thousand years of the human fascination with evil.* San Francisco: HarperSanFrancisco.

Menzies, W. C. (Director), Alperson, E. L. (Producer), Battle, J. T. (Story), & Blake, R. (Writer). (1953). *Invaders from Mars* [Motion picture]. United States: Twentieth Century-Fox Film Corporation (Distributor).

Nielsen, K. (1998). *Satan, the prodigal son?: A family problem in the Bible.* Sheffield: Sheffield Academic Press. (Original work published 1991).

Norman, R. E. (1979). *The decline and destruction of the Orion Empire.* (4 vols.). El Cajon, CA: Unarius Educational Foundation.

Parrinder, G. (1963). *Witchcraft: European and African.* (New ed.). London: Faber and Faber. (Original work published 1958).

Partridge, C. (2003). Understanding UFO religions and abduction spiritualities. In C. Partridge (Ed.), *UFO religions* (pp. 3-42). London: Routledge.

Partridge, C. (2006). The eschatology of Heaven's Gate. In K. G. Newport & C. Gribbin (Eds.), *Expecting the end: Millennialism in social and historical context* (pp.49-66). Waco, TX: Baylor University Press.

Peet, R., Born, B., Davis, M., Fehrer, K., Feinstein, M., Feldman, S., et al. (2003). *Unholy trinity: The IMF, World Bank and the WTO.* London: Zed Books.

Peters, T. (1995). Exo-theology: Speculations on extraterrestrial life. In J. R. Lewis (Ed.), *The gods have landed: New religions from other worlds* (pp. 187-206). Albany, NY: State University of New York Press.

Polanski, R. (Writer/Director), & Castle, W. (Producer). (1968). *Rosemary's baby* [Motion picture]. United States: Paramount Pictures.

Purkiss, D. (2000). *Troublesome things: A history of fairies and fairy stories.* London: Allen Lane.

Richardson, J. T., Best, J., & Bromley, D. G. (Eds.) (1991). *The satanism scare.* New York: A. de Gruyter.

Rilla, W. (Director), Kinnoch, R. (Producer), & Silliphant, S. (Writer). (1960). *Village of the damned* [Motion picture]. United States: Metro-Goldwyn-Mayer.

Robison, J. (1967). *Proofs of a conspiracy against all the religions and governments of Europe, carried on in the secret meetings of Free Masons, Illuminati, and reading societies: collected from good authorities.* Boston, MA: Western Islands. (Original work published 1797).

Ruppersberg, H. (1987). The alien messiah in recent science fiction films. *Journal of Popular Film and Television, 14* (4), 158-166.

Russell, C. (Writer/Director), Harris, J. H., & Harvey, R. (Producers), & F. Darabont (Writer). (1988). *The blob* [Motion picture]. United States: Palisades Entertainment.

Russell, J. B. (1977). *The Devil: Perceptions of evil from antiquity to primitive Christianity.* Ithaca, NY: Cornell University Press.

Russell, J. B. (1981). *Satan: The early Christian tradition.* Ithaca, NY: Cornell University Press.

Russell, J. B. (1986). *Mephistopheles: The Devil in the modern world.* Ithaca, NY: Cornell University Press.

Saliba, J. (2003). UFOs and religion: A case study of Unarius Academy of Science. In J. R. Lewis (Ed.), *Encyclopedic sourcebook of UFO religions* (pp. 191-208). Amherst, NY: Prometheus Books.

Schmoeller, D. (Director), Ljoka, D. (Writer/Producer), Schmoeller, G., & Matonak, R. (Producers). (1990). *The arrival* [Motion picture]. United States: Del Mar Entertainment.

Scott, R. (Director), Carroll, G., Giler, D., & Hill, W. (Producers), & O'Bannen, D. (Writer). (1979). *Alien* [Motion picture]. United States: Twentieth Century-Fox Film Corporation.

Segal, R. A. (2003). Jung on UFOs. In C. Partridge (Ed.). *UFO religions* (pp. 314-328). London: Routledge.

Sellon, E. B., & Weber, R. (1992). Theosophy and the Theosophical Society. In A. Faivre & J. Needleman (Eds.), *Modern esoteric spirituality* (pp. 311-329). New York: Crossroad.

Seymour, G. (2002a). *Reptilians.* Retrieved May 1, 2002, from:

http://www.abduct.com/irm.htm.

Seymour, G. (2002b). *The late Karla Turner speaks of reptilian atrocities.* Retrieved May 1, 2002, from:

http://www.abduct.com/irm.htm.

Showalter, E. (1997). *Hystories: Hysterical epidemics and modern culture.* New York: Columbia University Press.

Sitchin, Z. (1990). *Genesis revisited: Is modern science catching up with ancient knowledge?* New York: Avon.

Smith, S. G. (2003). Opening a channel to the stars: The origins and development of the Aetherius Society. In C. Partridge (Ed.), *UFO religions* (pp. 84-102). London: Routledge.

Snnody. (1999). *Deposits.* Retrieved August 26, 1999, from: http://www.heavensgatetoo.com/exitchk.htm.

Soltec (2003). *Ashtar Command and popular culture.* Retrieved March 24, 2003, from: http://spiritexpress.org/acc/home/acsoltec1.htm.

Spielberg, S. (Director/Producer), Kennedy, K. (Producer), & Mathison, M. (Writer). (1982). *E.T.: The extra terrestrial* [Motion Picture]. United States: Universal Pictures.

Stevenson, J. (Ed.) (1987). *A new Eusebius: Documents illustrating the history of the Church to AD 337.* (2nd ed.). London: SPCK. (Original work published 1968).

Strieber, W. (1987). *Communion: A true story: Encounters with the unknown.* London: Century.

Stupple, D. (1984). Mahatmas and space brothers: The ideologies of alleged contact with extraterrestrials. *Journal of American Culture, 7,* 131-139.

Thomas, K. (1973). *Religion and the decline of magic: Studies in popular beliefs in sixteenth- and seventeenth-century*

England. Harmondsworth: Penguin. (Original work published 1971).

Tingay, K. (2000). Madame Blavatsky's children: Theosophy and its heirs. In S. Sutcliffe & M. Bowman (Eds.), *Beyond New Age: Exploring alternative spiritualities* (pp. 37-50). Edinburgh: Edinburgh University Press.

Tingay, K. (2004). The Theosophical Society. In C. Partridge (Ed.), *Encyclopedia of new religions: New religious movements, sects and alternative spiritualities* (pp. 320-322). Oxford: Lion Publishing.

Tonkin, B. (2001). Entropy as demon: Buffy in Southern California. In R. Kaveney (Ed.), *Reading the Vampire Slayer: An unofficial critical companion to Buffy and Angel* (pp. 37-52). London: Tauris Parke.

Trachtenberg, J. (1943). *The Devil and the Jews: The medieval conception of the Jew and its relation to modern antisemitism.* New Haven, CT: Yale University Press.

Trachtenberg, J. (1970). *Jewish magic and superstition: A study in folk religion.* New York: Atheneum. (Original work published 1939).

Tuella (1982). *Project world evacuation; channeled by the Ashtar Command.* Deming, NM: Guardian Action Publications.

Tuella (1985). *Ashtar: A tribute.* Durango, CO: Guardian Action Publications.

Tumminia, D. (2003). When the archangel died: From revelation to routinization of charisma in Unarius. In C. Partridge (Ed.), *UFO religions* (pp. 62-83). London: Routledge.

Tumminia, D., & Kirkpatrick, R. G. (1995). Unarius: Emergent aspects of an American flying saucer group. In J. R. Lewis (Ed.), *The gods have landed: New religions from other worlds* (pp. 85-104). Albany, NY: State University of New York Press.

Vallée, J. (1969). *Passport to Magonia: From folklore to flying saucers.* Chicago: Henry Regnery.

Victor, J. S. (1993). *Satanic panic: The creation of a contemporary myth.* Chicago: Open Court.

Wachowski, A., & Wachowski, L. (Writers/Directors), & Silver, J. (Producer). (1989). *The matrix* [Motion picture]. United States: Warner Bros.

Wallis, R. (1974). The Aetherius Society: A case study in the formation of a mystagogic congregation. *Sociological Review, 22,* 27-44.

Warren, N. J. (Director), Gordon, R., & Speechley, D. (Producers), & Maley, G., & Maley, N. (Writers). (1981).

Inseminoid [Motion picture]. United Kingdom: Jupiter Films.

Wells, H. G. (1898). *The war of the worlds*. London: Heinemann.

Wenham, G. J. (1987). *Genesis 1-15*. Waco, TX: Word Books.

Westermann, C. (1994). *Genesis 1-11: A continental commentary* (J. J. Scullion, Trans.). Minneapolis, MN: Fortress Press. (Original work published 1972).

Whitmore, J. (2000). Abductees. In J. R. Lewis (Ed.), *UFOs and popular culture: An encyclopaedia of contemporary myth* (pp. 1-4). Santa Barbara, CA: ABC-Clio.

Wilcox, R. V., & Lavery, D. (Eds.). (2003). *Fighting the forces: What's at stake in "Buffy the Vampire Slayer"*. Lanham, MD: Rowman & Littlefield.

Winslade, J. L. (2002). Teen witches, wiccans, and "wanna-blessed-be's": Pop-culture magic in *Buffy the Vampire Slayer*. *Slayage: the On-line International Journal of Buffy Studies, 1*(1). Retrieved October 30, 2006, from: http://www.slayage.tv/essays/slayage1/winslade.htm.

Wright, N. G. (1996). Charismatic interpretations of the demonic. In A. N. S. Lane (Ed.), *The unseen world: Christian reflections on angels, demons and the heavenly realm* (pp. 149-163). Carlisle: Paternoster Press.

Yeaworth, I. S., (Director), Harris, J. H. (Producer), & T. Simonson & K. Phillips (Writers). (1958). *The blob* [Motion picture]. United States: Tonylyn Pictures.

University of
Chester

Inaugural and
Professorial
Lectures
2 0 0 4

Chester
Academic
Press

Chester Academic Press
Corporate Communications
University of Chester
Parkgate Road
Chester
CH1 4BJ
http://www.chester.ac.uk/academicpress/

Price £3.00

ISBN 1-905929-16-1

9 781905 929160 >